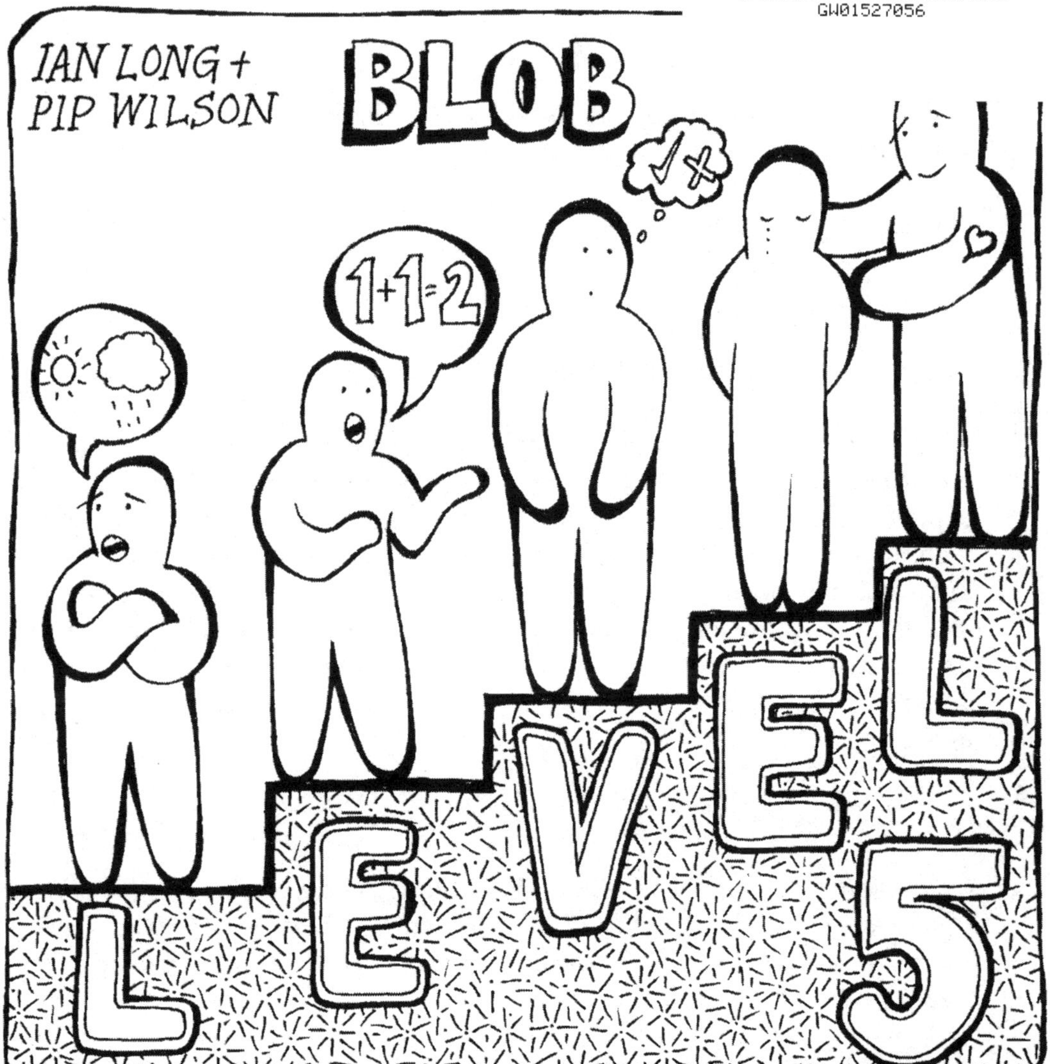
IAN LONG +
PIP WILSON
BLOB
1+1=2
LEVEL 5

Dedicated to all my beautiful relatives who change the world for the better, without being recognised

Published by www.blobtree.com

First published 2013

Copyright Ian Long and Pip Wilson 2013

All rights reserved. The whole of this work, including all text and illustrations, is protected by copyright. No part of it may be copied, altered, adapted or otherwise exploited in any way without prior express permission, unless it is in accordance with the provisions of the Copyright Designs and Patents Act 1988. No parts of this work may otherwise be loaded, stored, manipulated, reproduced or transmitted in any form or by any means, electronic or mechanical, including photocopying and recording, or by any information storage and retrieval system without prior written permission from the publisher, on behalf of the copyright owner.

ISBN: 978-1-291-54071-0

Other blobtree.com books include: Blob Angrr! Blob Life, The Big Book of Blobs, Blob Feelings, Blob Bible, Blob Lent, Blob Advent, Blob Book of Blob Trees, Blob Training Manual, You Are A Beautiful Human Person, Gutter Feelings, Between The Bars, Pip Wisdom and many more.

Our online shop to download Blobs is at www.blobtree.com

Con-tents

- Pip's Introduction
- Introduction - how to use this book - don't miss!
- Level 1 to Level 5 - words, images and exercises
- Applying Level 5
    - *Bullying*
    - *Spirituality*
- Level Zero - so many of us live at this level

To contact us about anything in this book, please message Ian at ilong@tiscali.co.uk and Pip can be contacted via his blog - www.pipwilson.com

Introduction by Pip Wilson

Gifts often come wrapped differently. Some BIG, small, delicately wrapped, in brown paper, glittery, shiny, tied in ribbons.

You are precious
valuable
special - in extreme
A GIFT
from G♡D
to this World
Community

You are a gift from G♡D and the worst thing is for you to stay unwrapped. You have so much to offer - and that is your uniqueness - difference - from every other person on the planet. If we unwrap - feel a bit naked, we grow. If we stay unwrapped, closed, unknown, unrevealed to others, we do not share our uniqueness - we take no risks.

I talk about Level 5 communication and I want to walk you through the levels.

Level 1 - cliché - is when we talk in clichés - 'lovely weather we are having' - so natural to say to strangers but so boring with intimate friends + those we wish to relate to better.

Level 2 - facts - this level is when we communicate facts only. Retelling what we have done, what we saw on TV, viewed at the football match. Interesting, maybe, but only for a little while.

Level 3 - opinions - this level we start to unwrap a little - it is when we give something of ourselves away (maybe about the TV programme or football). Watch out here - others could disagree.

Level 4 - feelings - is the big start of communication - unwrapping. Level 4 is all about feelings. When we are honest to another about our feelings which are active - here and now - right there in our interior self. How we are feeling within - emotional stuff. When we are willing to take that step, we reveal/unwrap - we are taking risks - but wonderfully so. People begin to see our beautiful humaness - we become more alive to them.

Level 5 - total openness - this is the target - may never be achieved. It is total openness, feelings, honesty - fully unwrapped. This, I believe, is beautiful. This is how all people best open up, grow, develop, change. And I believe that the better we become at this - the warmer, the more beautiful we can become - in our 'becoming'.

We can Level 5 with our partners, our friends, workmates, G♡D too!

It all begins with taking the risk - taking off wrappings - share the gift we are with others - not waiting for others...

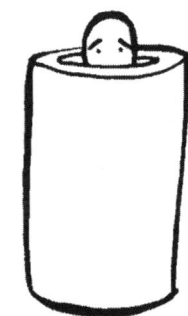

...or we can stay a gift unwrapped - a beautiful human 'being', a beautiful human 'becoming'.

You are much more than I can see...

Pip

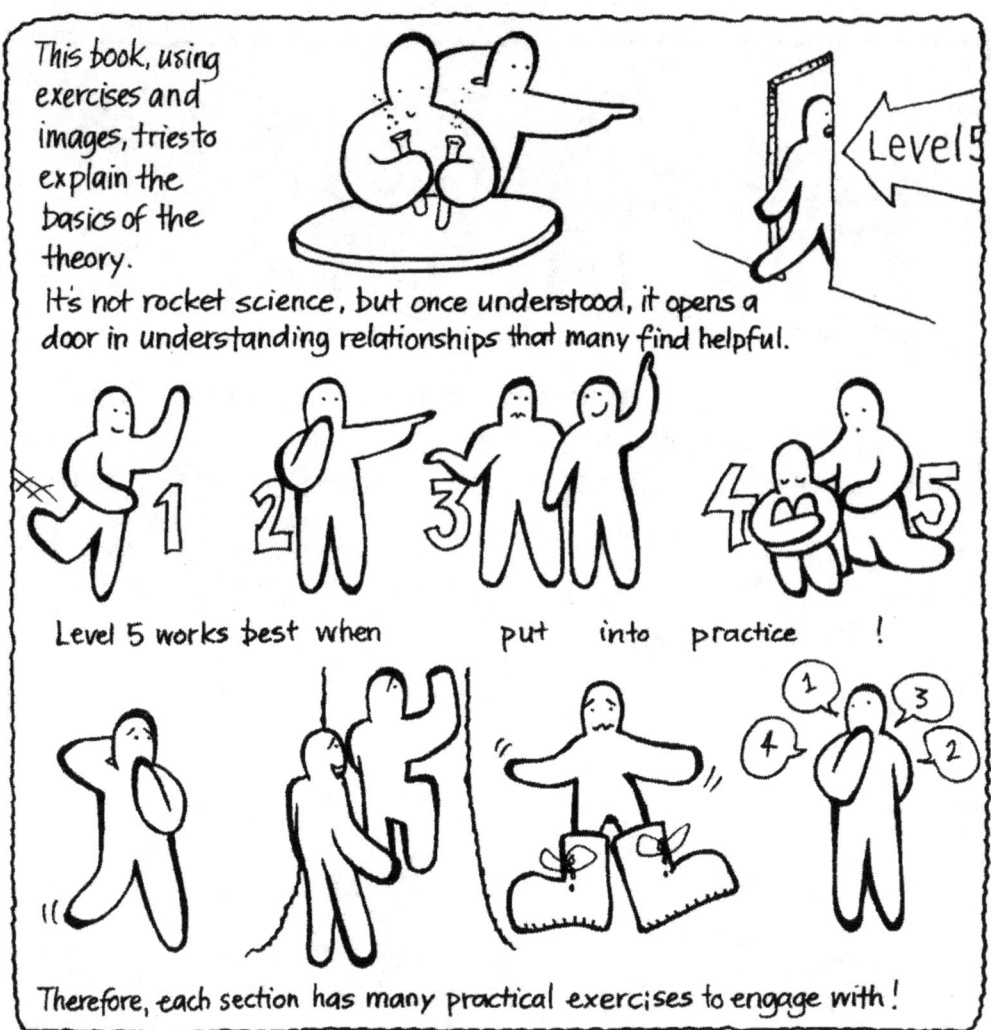

Level 1

Level 1: Cliches

This is a phase we use with strangers, and usually quickly pass through

Cliches can be as simple as 'Morning' or 'Alright mate',

a comment about the weather or a slap on the back

Car drivers often use L1 signals

When did you use L1 today?

Do we know people who talk to us in cliches all the time?

Are there people who use cliches all of the time?

Do you ever use cliches with your family?

Exercise 1

As you go through today, take note of each occasion someone uses L1 cliches with you, and the phrases we use in response.

Visual Exercise Look at the Level 1 situations below

Touch the Blobs that do the things you do in Level 1

Exercise 2

Think of a person who you constantly stay at L1 with? Is it your choice? Each time you meet, see if you can find a way to deepen the relationship.

Exercise 3

Are there any members of your extended family who you keep at Level 1? Each time you meet, reflect on why that might be.

Group Exercise

Find two other friends. Choose one to be the observer. The other two then try to have a chat using only Level 1 cliches. The observer should watch the body language and time how long it lasts. Swap over roles afterwards.

REFLECTIONS

Level 2: Exercises

Exercise 1
Each day, for a week, observe how many conversations involve sharing facts and information.

Only do one exercise at a time

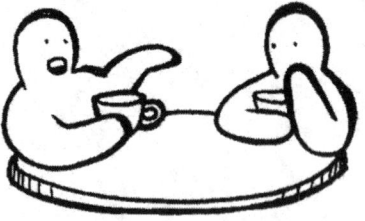

Exercise 2
Who talks to you primarily about facts? Facts can be about news, people, beliefs, clothes, etc.

Exercise 3
Who relates to you through facts from your family?

Exercise 4
Who are the people at work who only talk to you in facts?

Level 3: Opinions

Facts become interesting once we attach our own beliefs to them. Every election is based around such conflicts - right wing v left.

Friendships are often built around people who share our opinions.

Opposite opinions often result in conflicts.

Successful organisations use entirely opposing points of view to drive their vision.

Level 3: Organisations

Newspapers provide information within an overall point of view. Few organisations are independent, and are led by editorial opinion.

Parliaments across the world depend upon good arguments to persuade others. Discussion and debate are essential to a strong democracy... and we all have an opinion about the current Government!

Level 3: Questions

Do you enjoy listening to a variety of opinions... or do you prefer your own?

Are there opinions which annoy you?

Do you tend to prefer the opinions of men or women?

Do you enjoy taking time to form an opinion... or find making one fairly easy?

Do your opinions influence others?

Do you share similar opinions with friends?

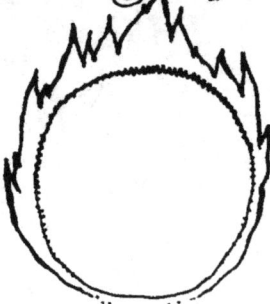

Level 3: Exercises

Exercise 1
Are there people who we always clash with? Study the event as it happens. Who usually ignites the conflict? How? How do we react? *Think - How can you break the pattern next time?*

Exercise 2
Who do you rarely get into arguments with? Is that because you generally agree, or because you are free to express your own point of view?

Exercise 3
Conflict often occurs within families. Who tends to 'wind you up' at family events? Is there anyone who manages to 'keep the peace'? How do they do it?

♫ Notes

Exercise 4

Each time you find yourself in an argument, note down what the theme of it was, who with, their age and gender.

Exercise 5

How does your boss like you to express your opinion? Is the inner circle made up of people who agree with the boss, or who broaden opinion?

Exercise 6

How do you react to new opinions? Do you listen carefully in order to be convinced or do you tend to defend your own point of view?

Level 3: Internet

The Internet used to be used as a quicker way to email. Now its got faster and more powerful, opinions are being freely given.

Places such as Twitter exist for everyone to vent their opinions, seconds after the latest news breaks... resulting in new crimes!

People have always voiced their opinions in a variety of inappropriate ways, but the Internet....

... enables the 'thought police' to correct our opinions... if we tweet them!

Level 3: Body Language

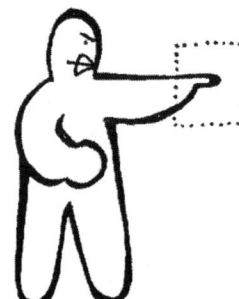

One of the key features of Level 3 is the pointing finger. It is a finger of accusation and judgement

Exercise: Try to have an argument with someone using open palms... it's hard!

So much of what is written in newspapers is in accusatory tones. The finger of judgement is pointed at people who are often innocent.

Pointing fingers usually point in both directions. If the intensity increases, fingers are replaced with weapons... the start of war.

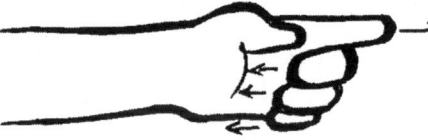

Many believe that when we point the finger of accusation at others, it often reveals something of our own guilt. We can use this as an exercise: the next time that we feel tempted to pass judgement on others, reflect whether we do a similar thing.

Level 4: Signals

Feelings are signals to us. They are one way that our body attempts to speak to us. Feelings, like thoughts and co-ordination, can be exercised and developed.

Have you ever stopped yourself from having an anger outburst?

Have you ever been to see a film on your own, just to see what loneliness feels like?

When you are next in conversation, notice when you feel an itch on your face. What triggered that feeling? Something said or thought?

When you next watch a film or TV programme, take note of the 'signals' in the body language of the actors.

Level 4: Exercises

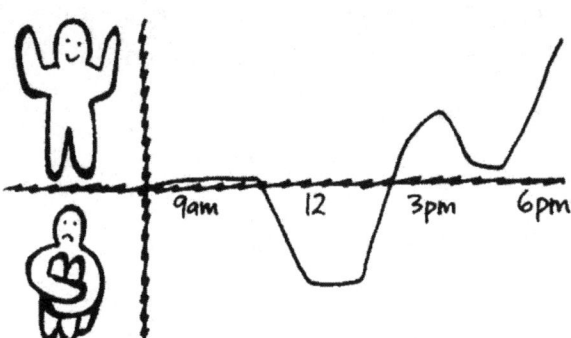

Exercise 1

During the day, at several set intervals, note down how you are feeling. Pop them onto a simple 'feelings graph'. Do this over a week and see if there are any patterns.

Exercise 2

Using the list of feelings words, or one of your own, circle all of the emotions that you pass through during a day/week. Are there feelings that you'd like to explore? Find ways to do that.

Feelings Word List

Excited	Peaceful
Ecstatic	Relaxed
Jubilant	Calm
Devastated	Unsure
Wounded	Troubled
Empty	Deceived
Offended	Confused
Jealous	Ridiculed
Fuming	Frustrated
Betrayed	Harassed
Shaken	Abused
Fearful	Afraid
Horrified	Shy
Respected	Determined
Encouraged	Hopeful
Loved	Energised
Distant	Discarded
Hurt	Upset
Lonely	Inadequate
Ashamed	Nervous
Cheerful	Good
Pleased	Valued

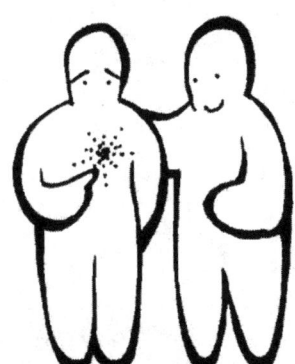

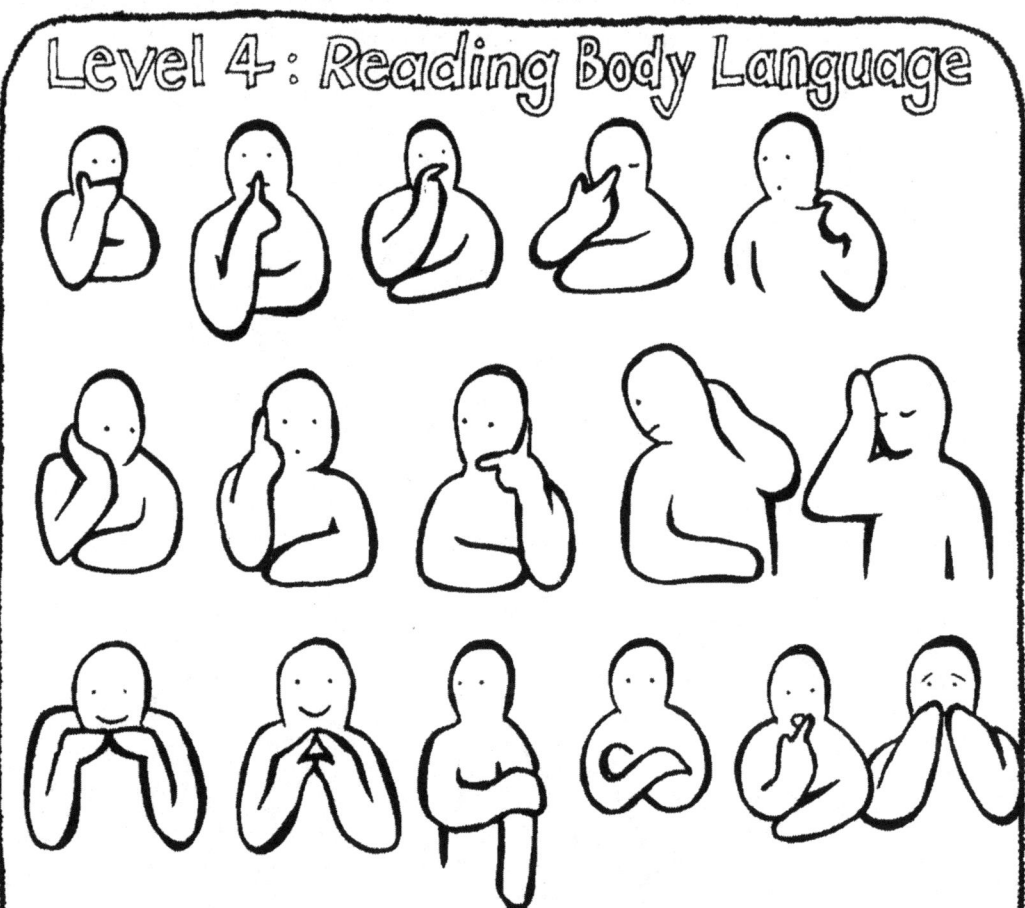

Level 4: Communicating in 3D

What is it that makes Level 4 so special?

When minds connect, at level 2 and 3, we make an important connection

Another dimension of communication is touch. Whether its a level 1 high 5, or a warm embrace from the one we love, touch matters so much.

When we add in our feelings, the way that we commune-icate is completed... 3D!

Level 5: Total openness

Level 5 is an aim

One which we may never achieve

It is about being vulnerable

Vulnerable with ourselves - being honest about our strengths and weaknesses

Vulnerable with our close friends, and those we love

Vulnerable with strangers, and even those who dislike us

Until we can accept who we are, in all of our uniqueness, it is hard to reveal our soul to others

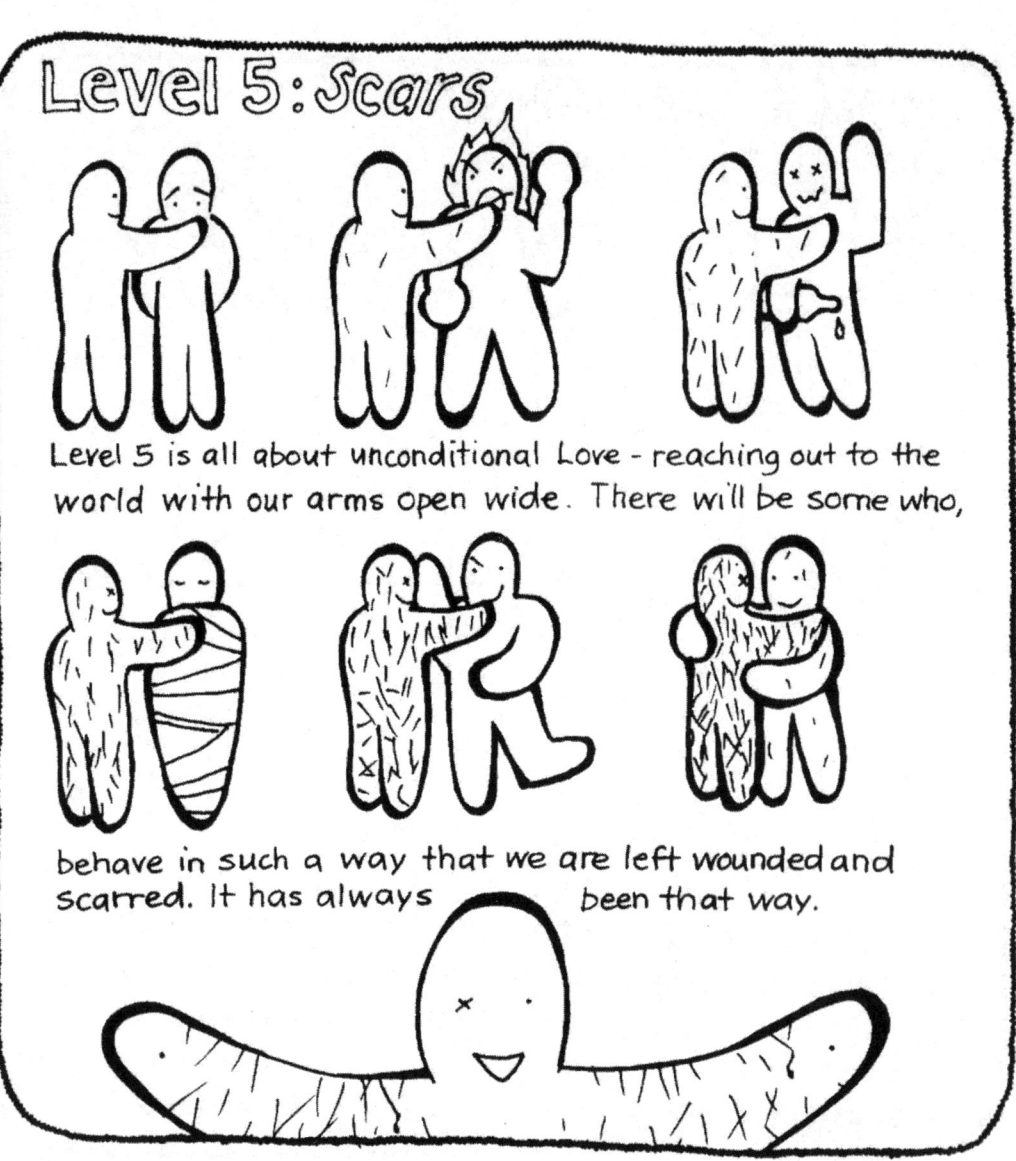

Level 5: Qualities

Being open to new ideas, new sensations, new experiences, new people

Love for those easy to Love and those with challenging behaviour

'The most beautiful people we have known are those who have known defeat, known suffering, known struggle, known loss and have found their way out of the depths. Beautiful people do not just happen.' *Elisabeth Kubler-Ross*

Level 5: Questions

Is there anyone who you would consider a L5 friend?

Would a L5 friend tempt you to consider being so vulnerable in life?

Is there anyone in your family who is open and vulnerable?

Have you ever had a painful L5 moment thrust upon you?

Who knows you the best - all your strengths and vulnerabilities?

Level 5: *Vulnerability*

Total openness is to put ourselves in a vulnerable position. It is like the trust that exists between a young child and their parents.

We often have to make ourselves vulnerable with doctors, counsellors, therapists and faith leaders.

To make ourselves vulnerable and to have that trust broken is devastating. Nothing is more painful, so many never make themselves vulnerable.

Being vulnerable will lead to being scarred, wounded and ignored at times - which is why few choose it as a way of life.

In order to cope with the L5 life, having others who live a vulnerable lifestyle is essential. We all need people who can support and encourage us. L5 friends.

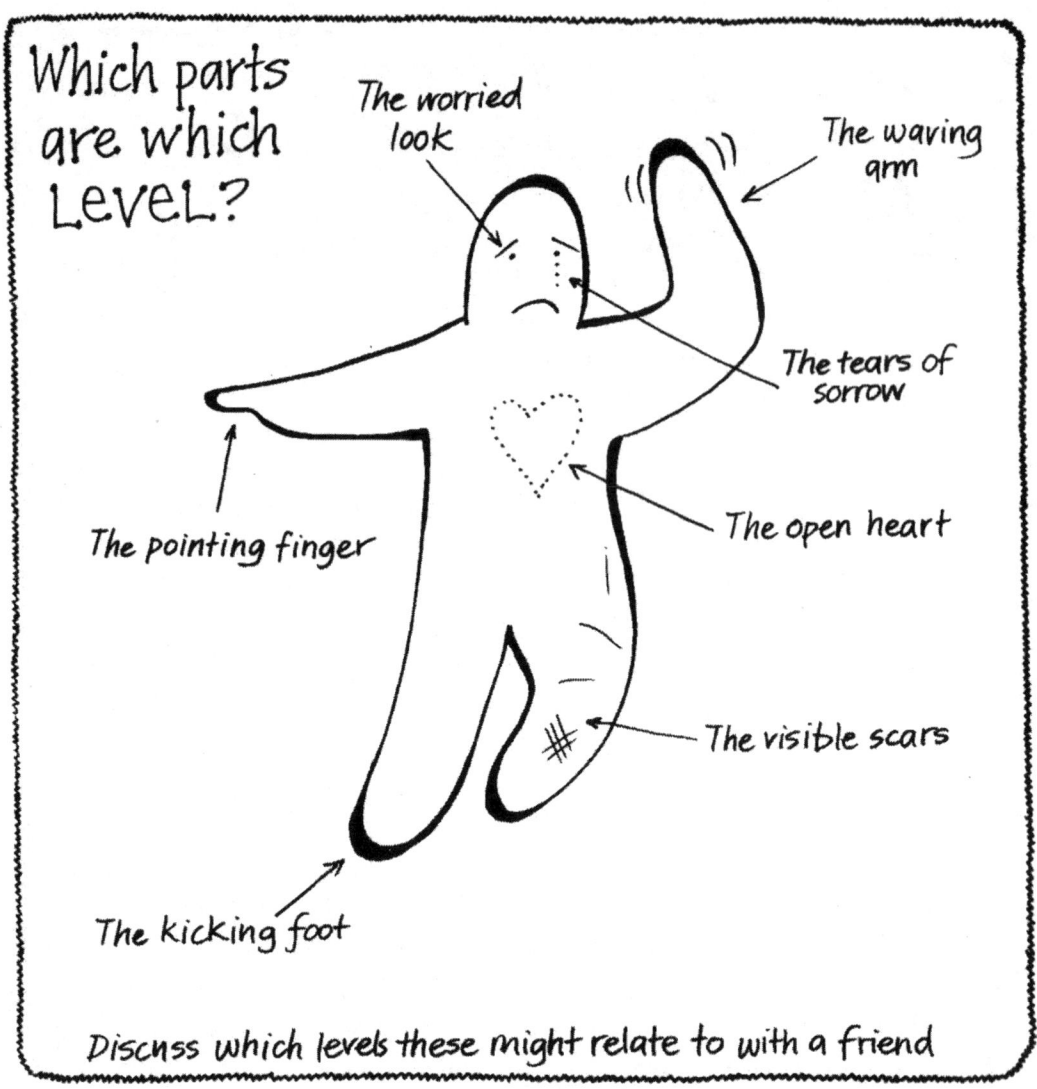

Questions to ask oneself - no right or wrong... self awareness

You are invited to a friend's home for the first time. Do you...
a: talk about the design of the building
b: find conversation difficult to begin with
c: find out how your friend is
d: express your opinion on the decor?

In a queue for a bus, do you...
a: find out how the next person is feeling
b: mention how long its taking to arrive
c: discuss the news
d: express your opinions on the news?

You are reading this book with a friend. Do you...
a: stop to talk about your opinion on what's written
b: put it down to discuss how you feel
c: add facts to what's been written
d: open up about something deep down?

Level 5: *reflections*

So you've got to this point in the book, having written your reflections, carried out the exercises and grasping L5... so what's next?

Level 5 isn't just a good read full of interesting ideas. It needs to be applied in your life in order for it to make sense. When Pip first introduced it to me, I began to use it.

As a young adult I used to get into lots of squabbles over L3 opinions. Over time I began to spot this and move onto L4 quickly. Instead of wanting to win arguments, I wanted to Love... a big change.

Living at L4 is so much more productive, I've found.

As a teacher in school, I noticed that facts, opinions and feelings play such a big part in how each child learns. The more relaxed they are, the quicker they learn.

Each year I worked hard to create a positive atmosphere in each lesson. Soon almost all children felt able to share. Those who were shy were given a talk-partner.

Some children reminded me of myself - spotting my occasional mistakes. I expect they found fault with all adults. It seemed to make them feel superior.

Rather than humiliate them by pointing out their mistakes, I discussed how they would feel if they had their mistakes pointed out to others. Usually this stopped their behaviour.

In the remainder of this book, we'll look at how I applied Pip's concept of Level 5 to bullying, prayer... and provide exercises!

REFLECTION SPACE

Think of a situation/relationship where things need to improve. Where is it stuck at? L2/3/4?

Bullying happens at all stages of life. It can begin within the family, when siblings or parents bully a child.

Many workers suffer daily bouts of bullying. Because so much of it occurs in offices, bullies seem to thrive.

Even towards the end of life, the elderly can be picked on by their aggressive family members.

By understanding how bullies tend to operate, we can change from being a victim, and stand up for ourselves. Once that occurs, we can help other targets.

Level 1 bullying can be seen in aggressive looks, being blanked-out as someone walks down a corridor past you, or the odd thump and nasty name that lingers for days after. Over a prolonged period of time, these things alone can result in signs of depression.

Level 2 bullying tends to occur when others pick on us using facts - our 'underperformance', our poor use of language, our clothing and our skills. Performance management can be used by bullies under a professional disguise. Parents often use differences between siblings to pick on one continuously.

Level 3 bullying can often be hidden to us. We may never find out about what others have said against us. Those who bully us may 'poison the minds' of our colleagues, friends and even our family. Doors remain closed. Friendships suddenly end. Opinions are like an invisible wall - one which many minorities feel on a daily basis.

L4 bullying really hurts. It burrows away into our feelings. It can belittle us, make us feel truly incapable, lead to long-term sickness, depression and inadequacy. We need to fight it!

Ways to deal with bullying on all Levels

Most bullies haven't selected their victims, it's just that the victim doesn't fight back. If a bully picks on us with verbal or physical cliches we need to move straight to Level 4 - "I don't like the way that you speak to me", or "I don't like the way that you touched me." If it stops, all well and good, but if the bully continues, then we need to get support. They need to know that they are in the minority. For most situations, this will be enough.

There are situations though where this is difficult. In a long term abusive relationship over many years, sometimes the only way to end the bullying is to end the relationship. This will take support, but may be essential for our health.

For over 6 billion beautiful humans, spirituality plays an important part in their daily life. Hindus, Muslims, Christians, Jews, Sikhs, Buddhists and all the smaller faith groups have at their heart a relationship - betweens humans and the Creator.

Level 5 comes into play in every relationship

It is seen most clearly through meditation and prayer

In each faith there are those who feel safest to pray within set guidelines... or freely!

Level 5 gives us an insight into the way people pray.

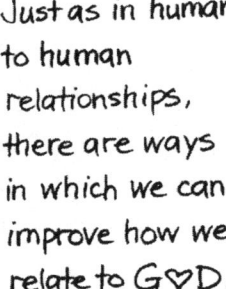

Just as in human to human relationships, there are ways in which we can improve how we relate to G♡D.

Level 1 Prayer

What do you consider this to be? In any relationship, even with G♡D, it involves cliches. For some of us that may involve us saying the same prayer, day after day.

Level 1 prayer generally involves a one-way conversation - us talking to G♡D. It tends to rely upon rituals and repetition.

None of it is wrong, just like all of L1 chat. Its just that there is so much more!

It is without creativity...

... and more to do with our appearance.

Level 3: Prayer

One of the most 'interesting' moments when people pray together is when different opinions arise.

Feelings and opinions can be very opposing and the whole group can get drawn in to the 'prayerful argument'!

Some decide to express opinions against situations happening to them, during prayer. There is a long tradition of this begun by the Psalmists.

How do we resolve prayer arguments?

Level 3: Faith and opinions

Wherever there are opinions, there is a tendency for conflict.

In Islam, the different factions are at war. In Christianity it used to be war between Catholics + Protestants.

All faiths have had differences which have resulted in wars. This has been true for athiest beliefs too.

The Crusades, Communism, the Shia/Sunni conflict, and all other religious/athiest conflicts have been a heady mixture of opinion fuelled by feelings.

Some of the best examples of conflict resolution in the last 100 years have involved faith at L4 and L5 – moving beyond opinions.

Nelson Mandela's faith shone through after his release when he set up 'Peace + Reconciliation' hearings to heal South Africa.

Level 5: Prayer

The greatest role models in each faith demonstrated intimacy in their prayer life.

Their relationship with G♡D was so clear, that they could hear G♡D's voice.

This led to new ways of living, new ways to Love, and new communities.

All of the key teachers in each faith have had moments when their lives have been 'awakened' at a heart level — Level 5.

The challenge for each faith is to remain in that place of freshness + intimacy.

Level 0: Spirituality

Often people who are confident at expressing themselves in all Levels 1 to 4, struggle to come alive spiritually.

Where people struggle, they are often surrounded by friends who also struggle in their spirituality.

motion leads to emotion

There are so many ways to discover a personal faith. The first step involves moving. Motion leads to e-motions!

Find someone who has a relationship with G♡D and ask them to teach you how to discover G♡D for yourself. C.S. Lewis was guided by J.R.R. Tolkien.

Level 0

▷ Some people don't even get a 'good morning' come their way. They are passed by on the streets. For a country which previously used to acknowledge everyone, we now play 'averting our eyes'.

We can ignore those who depend on us...

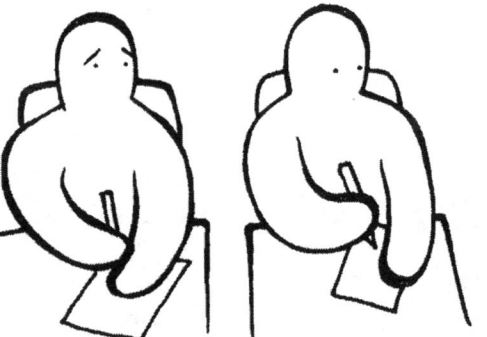

We can be ignored by colleagues...

feel distant in our intimate relationships...

Level Zero moments:

Bullying - putting up our defences to protect ourselves

Total exhaustion

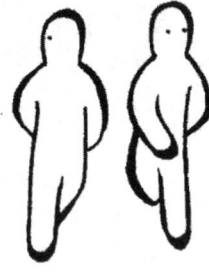

Passing strangers in the street

Sitting next to strangers in a surgery waiting room, avoiding eye contact

Sitting in front of a screen, passively watching

Sitting, unable to think, speak or do anything

Lz Level zero is a state O

of Withdrawal...

How to teach a group Level 5

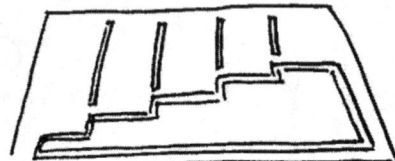

Layout masking tape on the floor of the hall in the manner shown above - steps and each section separated by a line.

As everyone comes in, explain the basic concept and five key words. Then get the group to stand in L1 and challenge them to talk in cliches for two minutes. You will probably need to agree what cliches are! Discuss how hard this is, but that it is usually the level that conversations start at between strangers.

Move everyone into Level 2. Explain that this is where we talk facts. Give pairs two minutes each to give facts about themselves, their likes and dislikes. After two minutes, swap over. Discuss how this was much easier than Level 1! This is often the level we relate to certain groups in our lives - professionals, the police, teachers, etc. Ask if anyone had a fact-based conversation earlier today.

Introduce Level 3 using a summary from the book, emphasising the key word 'opinion'. Using a topical issue from the news, get pairs to discuss their views. After a few minutes, ask them to carry on, but using open palms, rather than pointing fingers. Reflect upon how this change affected them.

Before moving onto Level 4, reflect with the group about the day. When have they used the first three levels during their day? Get some to share with the whole group before encouraging the pairs to talk again.

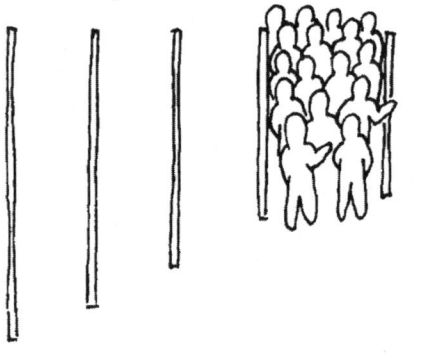

For Level 4, explain the key word, 'feelings'. Get the group to think of the last time they felt positive / excited, and the last time they felt disappointed. In the pairs, share these experiences. Reflect upon how you, as an observer, noticed different body language. Ask the group about how they felt sharing. Explain that when we share our feelings it creates a climate of greater trust and openness.

Explain to the group that Level 5 is a place of complete trust and openness. It goes beyond just sharing feelings, it is to be very vulnerable. As such, it tends to happen between intimate friends over years.

Get pairs to reflect upon how they could use this in their lives.

There are many other ways to enhance this learning, but by using an experiential approach, most will recall 'Level 5' for years to come. This exercise can be carried out on a beach or a field if there are no halls big enough for your group.

REFLECTIONS